AUTISM AFTER THE PANDEMIC

James Ball, EdD, BCBA-D
Kristie Brown-Lofland, MS, CCC-A

Foreword by Temple Grandin, PhD

A Step-by-Step Guide Back to School & Work

DEDICATION

Throughout our careers, we have had the privilege of working with many individuals on the spectrum and their amazing families. However, two young men are special to us and will forever live in our hearts—Austin and Everett Colclasure.

We began working with Austin when he was a preschooler and we have watched him grow over the years. Even though he has experienced many challenges in his life, Austin has never ceased to amaze us. He is a loving soul and continues to enhance our lives and those around him.

Everett is Austin's champion and younger brother. His care and understanding of his older brother are unmatched. Together they have enriched our lives and inspire us to do what we do every day.

This is Austin and Everett with their Mom and Dad enjoying their "new normal" time together.

AUTISM AFTER THE PANDEMIC
A Step-by-Step Guide Back to School & Work

All marketing and publishing rights guaranteed to and reserved by:

FUTURE HORIZONS INC.
(800) 489-0727
(817) 277-0727
(817) 277-2270 (fax)
E-mail: info@fhautism.com
www.fhautism.com

ISBN: 978-1-949177-58-9

Contents

Foreword

The autism spectrum is broad: people on the spectrum range from the computer scientists in Silicon Valley to non-verbal adults who may have difficulty dressing themselves. Jim Ball and Kristie Brown Lofland's book is ideal for both verbal and nonverbal children and adults who have low verbal abilities. If a diagnosis or services are not available, this book is the ideal "how-to guide" that enables you to begin working with your individual with autism now. If a three- or four-year-old child is not talking, the worst things that parents can do is to do nothing. It is essential to start working with the child now. Younger children need many hours of instruction to learn language.

There is a tendency to underestimate the abilities of non-verbal individuals; Dr. Ball has worked with many adults, often referring to his work with a particular non-verbal adult who needed help to learn a job. Succeeding at his job made this individual feel good about having a purpose in life: he went from doing almost nothing to becoming the coffee specialist at the local convenience store. People appreciated his ability to make really good coffee, and he enjoyed his new identity as the coffee man. When he retired, he continued to serve coffee in a local nursing home. Teachers, parents, and professionals need to have the attitude of looking at what a person can learn instead of looking at what they cannot do.

The first tip in *Autism After the Pandemic* is "no surprises." Surprises scare people with autism. If a child or an adult is going to a new school or job, visiting before they start is highly recommended. This book has step-by-step instructions for teaching skills and strategies to prevent meltdowns, learn new skills, and to cope and grow in a work or school environment, and it is a valuable resource in families returning to a "new normal."

— Temple Grandin,
Author of *The Way I See It* and *The Loving Push*

Introduction

We have arrived at a new normal: life after the arrival of COVID-19. How do we help those with developmental and/ or intellectual disabilities and those on the autism spectrum return to school or adult services? It has been a long haul at home! Both children and adults are used to the home environment and routines. Some students have been out of their school/adult program for months. It is now time to go back to the normal school/work routine, but what does that "normal" mean? Schedules and structure are different, and learning has been interrupted, yet hopefully maintained. How do parents prepare their child to transition back to school or work? This workbook will outline the strategies that should be put in place prior to your child going back to their school or adult services placement. Each strategy will be explored in depth and followed by instructional examples, so you and the individual with autism who you're supporting will be prepared for a successful first day when returning to school or an adult program.

Let's get started.

Schedules

The most important strategy is the use of schedules. This helps the individual you're working with understand the expectations of the environment: they know what is going to happen next and can predict the future. It can start with a simple one-item schedule and transform into the use of an electronic device to keep track of their day(s). It is important to remember that when the individual "gets" whatever schedule they are on, it is time to up the ante and make the system more sophisticated.

We all use some type of schedule in our own lives; using one for the person with autism will let them know what is expected of them and what they may be earning for following the schedule. This schedule should consist of pictures with the written word under each picture, or just the written word (if the person can read). The person with autism should have some choice in what the schedule looks like. For example, if we know we have four assignments we need to get done, we can put out the assignments and ask the person which one they want to do first, second, etc. This will allow them to have some say in the order of the things that need to be done. Because they often have such little choice in their lives, it is important that they be allowed to assist with their schedule.

To prepare for transitioning, it is critical to use a calendar. If you know when the individual will be going back to school or work, you can place a special sticker or icon on the calendar to signify the first day. It may be helpful to have the individual count the days down until they will be going to school or work. They can cross off or put a special sticker on each day in anticipation for the first day back.

The schedule can include, but is not limited to*:

- Written word, with or without pictures

- Pictures (actual/artificial)

- Objects

* This is dependent upon the child's overall ability level.

PARENT CHECKLIST

☑ *Pick the appropriate schedule (pictures, written word, or a combination)*

☑ *Organize the schedule*

☑ *When the task is complete, remove or cross off the picture or word*

☑ *Start with new schedule after completion*

Please reference Recommended Resources 1, to 3 at the back of the book.

EXAMPLES:

Morning Schedule

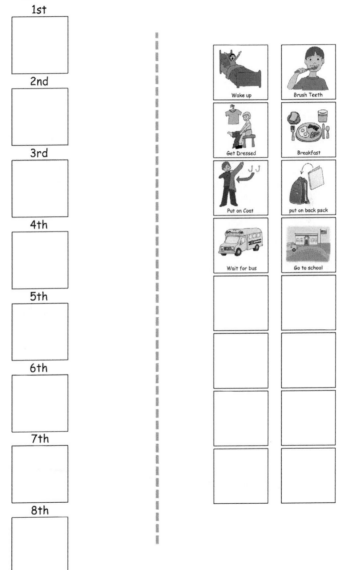

Schedule

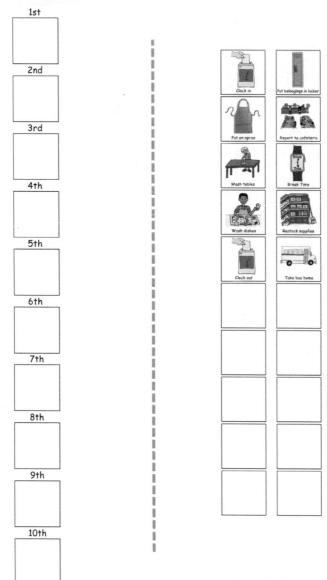

(Images created by K. Brown Lofland)

Social
Narratives

Social narratives are visual or written stories that describe social situations and the appropriate behaviors in these scenarios. They are used to help individuals with autism spectrum disorder (ASD) acquire and use appropriate social skills.

For example, Olivia's parents wrote a social narrative to use when running errands or leaving the house. Often, they would reread it (or part of it) before getting out of the car, when they anticipated Olivia's "want meter" was running high. Their narrative includes concrete strategies for Olivia to use if she feels frustrated to the point of hitting. As an example, while riding in the car, Olivia sees the McDonald's sign and wants chicken nuggets. Dad says "no," and reminds her that they are going to have dinner at home. Mom offers her a choice of two other workable alternatives, saying, "We can't go to McDonald's today, but you can have a choice for dinner. You can have chicken tenders or a cheesy ham sandwich." If Olivia's behavior continues to escalate, they remind Olivia of the self-control strategies that were previously taught to her: "Olivia, calm down. Take ten deep breaths," or "Olivia, nice hands. Close your eyes and think of the waves on the beach." The narrative also mentions that sometimes what Olivia wants might not be immediately available, and she will have to wait. For instance, instead of giving in to Olivia's negative behaviors, Dad can tell Olivia that the family will go to dinner at McDonald's the next day.

When using a social narrative with a nonverbal child, build include actual pictures in the appropriate social sequence or use a video model of appropriate behavior you want to see. If your social narrative is focused on eating with utensils, show the individual a picture sequence or a video model of using a fork rather than a prompting verbally.

PARENT CHECKLIST

☑ *Identify one social skill that needs to be addressed*

☑ *Write the social narrative with or without pictures*

☑ *Read the narrative with the individual prior to the activity*

☑ *Read the narrative on more than one occasion when necessary*

☑ *Positively reward the individual when he or she appropriately uses the social skill*

EXAMPLE:

When I Get Frustrated: Social Narrative

Sometimes when I go out with my family, I get frustrated when I cannot have what I want or do not get to have a choice. Sometimes what I want is not available when I want it, and I may have to wait. This may make me frustrated, too. It is okay to get frustrated, but it is not okay to hit.

The next time I get frustrated, I will try to:

1. Say "I'm frustrated."

2. Clap my hands or stomp my feet.

3. Take ten deep breaths.

4. Pick another offered choice.

Making an appropriate choice will keep me calm and make my family happy.

Please reference Recommended Resources 4 to 8 at the back of the book.

Video
Modeling

Video modeling is an instructional teaching technique that utilizes assistive technology and videos as the primary vehicle. It is a strategy that we have personally begun to use exclusively with the individuals we work with, regardless of ability or age.

Video modeling has a growing research base and can be used to teach a variety of skills, such as social skills, play skills, and many others. It is critical that parental/guardian permission be acquired in writing prior to starting any video modeling.

Video modeling has three core components:

1. Create or find a video acting out the target behavior. These can be made by recording the learner (or someone else) performing the target behavior; alternatively, commercially made videos are available online or for purchase.

2. Use the video to teach the skill.

3. Have the individual perform the skill.

PARENT CHECKLIST

☑ *Pick the skill*

☑ *Tape the video, or find an existing video*

☑ *Put it on a loop (Looper, Shadow Puppet, etc. are useful apps)*

☑ *Play it multiple times*

Please reference Recommended Resources 9 and 10 at the back of the book.

Repetition

People with an ASD or developmental disability love to learn through repetition, and may need a lot of it. Therefore, it should be a cornerstone to any programming, especially with recreational and leisure activities. These individuals may need multiple opportunities to try each new skill, and it may take a long time for individuals with ASD to get comfortable in their environment before they can enjoy some activities. It is critical that you stay as consistent and predictable as possible, and the best way to achieve this is through repetition. In combination with scheduling, it is the perfect way to allow the individual to understand expectations and predict what is going to happen next. This reduces stress and anxiety and helps the individual learn and establish new routines, so they will feel comfortable when returning to their school or place of work.

PARENT CHECKLIST

☑ *Start the activity*

☑ *Repeat*

☑ *Repeat*

☑ *Repeat*

EXAMPLE:

Hand-Washing Schedule

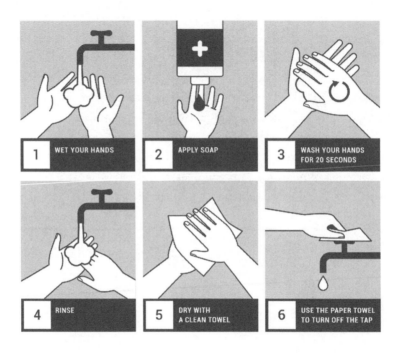

Give the individual the verbal cue "wash hands," then nonverbally prompt him/her to follow the visual. Do the activity as many times as possible without boring you or the person you're working with. Attempt to do activities in the time they would naturally occur (i.e., washing hands before eating, after going to the bathroom, etc.). Start and end the same way. Break up the opportunities throughout the day, getting as many repetitions in as possible. For individuals who require more repetition, create two to three opportunities to perform the task in a row. Do not forget to positively reinforce the learner when they are successful!

Please reference Recommended Resource 11 at the back of the book.

Safe Place/Person in School or Work

I f the individual does not already have a safe place or person in their school or place of work, a decision from the team needs to confirm this place or person. If social distancing is in place, the education team or service team could interact with one another through a virtual meeting. Once the safe person or place is established, a conversation should be had with the individual with autism prior to returning to school or work. A protocol on how the safe person or place is to be used should also be determined. For example, a system could be established where the individual has a pre-specified amount of break cards that allow him/her to leave an environment where they are not comfortable or are beginning to feel anxious. From there, a protocol should be designed describing exactly what will happen: where will the individual go, or who will they seek out? The safe place should in an open area that has clear visual boundaries (i.e., tape on the floor). A calming corner or safe place could have pillows, calming sensory tools, or even a weighted blanket. The safe place could have visuals that represent the choices the individual may select from in order to calm.

There may be occasions where the individual is not able to use this type of system. When this occurs, he or she should just be kept safe in any way possible; this is not a teachable moment. There should be a definition of antecedent behaviors that lead to a potential meltdown. If the person with autism begins to display these behaviors, the staff person should direct him or her to the safe place or safe person. This can be done using visuals and/or a social narrative.

Safe spaces can be a great calming strategy for autism meltdowns. For some people, a safe person may go with them to their calm-down corner to help them relax. For others, the individual will need space to be alone to calm down. This will be person-specific and determined depending on the needs of each person.

PARENT CHECKLIST

☑ *Establish the safe place/person*

☑ *Direct individual to safe place/person prior to escalation*

☑ *Use when necessary*

☑ *Praise the individual when he or she uses the safe place*

EXAMPLE:

Safe Place Social Story

When I am feeling anxious or getting upset, I may go to my safe place (the resource room, in the back of my classroom, etc.). Before I go to my safe place, I will place a break card on my desk so my teacher or supervisor will know where I am going.

In my safe place, I can choose a calming strategy. I will set the time for five minutes and choose from my calming menu:

- Sit on bean bag or rocking chair

- Use a body curl up

- Do five chair **pushups**

- Spend five minutes in the quiet **tent**

- Spend five minutes listening to music with headphones

When I get upset.....

☐ When I get upset

☐ take a break

☐ stop

☐ breathe

☐ think

☐ talk to the teacher

Break cards

Break cards

Calm Down Area

Please reference Recommended Resources 12 to 14 at the back of the book.

Chaining

S haping and chaining are often referred to in tandem, but they are different techniques. Whereas shaping is usually used when teaching one specific skill or aspect of a skill, chaining is a strategy that encompasses an entire sequence of behaviors or actions that, when put together, make up a complex skill. For example, chaining is used to teach skills such as self-help, personal care, and domestic chores (e.g., toothbrushing, hand washing, or face washing). Chaining involves breaking down a skill into its component parts and teaching each step in the chain until the individual can perform the entire task. There are two types of chaining: forward and backward. In forward chaining, we start with the first step in the process and build from there. In backward chaining, it is just the opposite: we start with finished skill and proceed from there.

PARENT CHECKLIST

☑ *Start the program*

☑ *Move to next step when the individual is independent (no prompts) in performing the step you are on*

☑ *Repeat above step until the program is complete*

☑ *Praise the individual for success*

EXAMPLE:

Forward Chaining

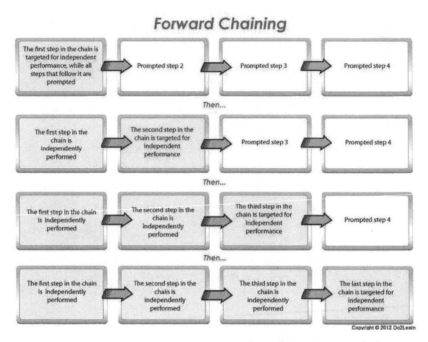

Copyright 2012 Do2Learn, do2learn.com

Forward Chaining of Wearing a Face Mask

1. Place face mask in hands with the inside of the mask facing you

2. Put the face mask over your chin, mouth, and nose

3. Place the elastic bands behind both of your ears. If you have ties instead of elastic, tie them behind your head tightly

4. Adjust the mask to cover chin, mouth, and nose

If necessary, add pictures to each of the steps.

Please reference Recommended Resources 15 and 16 at the back of the book.

Video Meeting
with Staff

Y ou and the individual with autism have probably already experienced some type of video platform meeting. If your child is doing e-learning while school is not in session, then he or she is utilizing some type of technology to complete their schoolwork. If you are working with an adult, he or she could be video conferencing with their staff at the adult center, with coworkers at their job, or just with friends. Prior to the beginning of the upcoming work or school year, there should be a meeting to go over the individual's behavior plan and/or reinforcement system. This meeting could be very brief, yet productive, so that you as a family can provide the structure and strategies to support the individual as they go back to school or their work setting. This meeting will enable the individual to be more prepared and therefore reduce their anxiety.

If possible, a video "meet and greet" with any of the upcoming school or work staff would be beneficial in reducing the individual's anxiety. In addition, a video could be made showing the school or work building, areas where the individual will be attending class or working, etc.

This is an opportunity to obtain any information to simulate a typical school or workday. Any video models would be helpful to show changes in the classroom/work environment.

PARENT CHECKLIST

☑ *Schedule meeting with staff*

☑ *Discuss pertinent information (behavior plan, schedule, etc.)*

☑ *Obtain visuals or video modeling recordings that are used at school or work*

☑ *Anticipate any changes (environmental, staff, etc.)*

EXAMPLE:

Visual of classroom distancing

Visual of boundary around chair

Reinforcement/
Motivational
System

The most critical aspect of any program is motivation: keeping people engaged and wanting to learn. How do we entice someone to build a relationship, complete a task, or learn a skill, especially during those times when all they want to do is what they want to do? We keep motivation and engagement active through the regular use of meaningful reinforcement. Remember that reinforcement is very individual, and even though there may be a system of motivation in a classroom or workplace, that does not mean that the individual on the spectrum is going to "buy into it" initially. Our goal is for him/her to use that system. In the beginning, we may need to implement another, more individualized system to motivate him or her; however, we are always working toward that classroom/workplace system.

The system you use at home should mirror the one that the individual's school or adult service agency has been using.

PARENT CHECKLIST

☑ *Get the exact motivational system from school/work*

☑ *Implement with consistently during simulated school/workday*

☑ *Give choices when appropriate*

☑ *Praise the individual when they are using appropriate behavior*

EXAMPLE:

first   then

put on shoes   play with tablet

Establish Routines in Advance: Simulate a Typical Day

E stablishing routines in advance is by far the most important step in the process of getting an individual ready for the return to their school or work program. Two to three weeks prior to school or work starting, simulate a school/work day.

Many children will display some difficulty separating from parents to attend school. The behaviors shown by the child could include tantrums when separating, problems sleeping alone, or refusal to attend school without parents. Some shyness or worry about schedules, schoolwork, or friends is natural during the back-to-school transition.

1. A week or two before school or work begins, start preparing your individual for the upcoming transition by getting back to school/ work routines (set times for bed, selecting tomorrow's clothes, etc.).

2. Create a school/work morning routine and practice it prior to the start of the first day. Begin waking up your individual a little earlier each morning, so that he or she is acclimated to the new wake-up time before returning to school or work.

3. Begin getting your individual up and be done with their morning routine prior to the time when school/work would begin. For example, if school or works starts at 8:00 a.m., have the person complete their school/work routine at 8:00 a.m.

4. Stay on a schedule and simulate as many transitions as possible.

5. Use the individual's motivational system as it would be used in their school/work environment.

6. Stay as close to the schedule as possible.

7. Visit the school or workplace before the school year begins or before returning to work. You may want to practice drop-off and pick-up routines.

8. Come up with a prize or a rewarding activity that a child could earn for separating from mom or dad to attend school.

9. Validate the individual's worry by acknowledging that, like any new activity, starting school or going back to work can be hard but soon becomes easy.

10. Talk to your individual frequently about what to expect when they return to school or work. This is a simple way to help reduce your individual's anxiety.

11. Crossing days off the calendar may help your individual to better understand when school or work starts again.

12. Take a virtual tour of the school, if possible. This can be arranged with your child's school team. While you might not get to meet your child's new teacher this early, at least your child will become familiar with the building prior to attending.

13. Take pictures of the school and personnel and incorporate them into a social narrative so that you and your child can review it prior to returning. You may be able to find these pictures on the school's website.

14. If your individual uses an augmentative device to communicate, make sure the device is charged and in good working condition.

15. If your individual has sensory issues, make sure he or she has a favorite sensory item available for the first day.

These suggestions can have a large positive effect on the individual's behavior, and will reduce everyone's anxiety. Therefore, it is so important that you are as consistent as possible.

PARENT CHECKLIST

☑ *Start two to three weeks prior to school/work starting*

☑ *Stay consistent*

☑ *Stick to the schedule, no matter what!*

☑ *Use a safe place if necessary*

☑ *Stay positive!*

Anticipate Their Sensory Needs and Be Prepared

Sensory needs are going to be specific for each individual; you should have established routines for their sensory needs already. In this section, we are looking at what changes your individual with autism might encounter in going back to school or their work setting. Your individual might have to wear a mask at school or their work center; it is critical that you get your child used to wearing this type of device before they return. As time goes on, there may be other restrictions that schools or adult work centers may require. Try to keep informed of those changes, so you can prepare your individual for any changes they will encounter in their school or work environment.

"Pairing" and "shaping" are two strategies that would help assist with wearing masks and adapting to new routines.

Pairing is the introduction of an unfamiliar object (such as the face mask) paired with positive reinforcers. For example, before we ask the person on the spectrum to wear the mask, we would have them hold the mask and reinforce them with praise and high-fives.

Shaping is the reinforcement of each step toward wearing the mask. First, the person would hold the mask, and we reinforce. Next, ask the person to bring the mask toward their face, and reward them. Once the individual has graduated to placing the mask onto their face, reward them again. Follow this process for each step: allowing the elastic to be put behind their ears, etc., until the person is wearing the mask. This may take several trials for each individual step. Try not to move ahead too quickly.

The following websites contain social narratives and visual supports on wearing a mask and/or how COVID-19 will affect school and/or work.

PARENT CHECKLIST

☑ *Schedule sensory breaks*

☑ *Have brain breaks (Go Noodle, Adventures to Fitness, etc. are all fun apps to use)*

☑ *Break as often as needed, but return to schedule ASAP and pick up where you left off*

EXAMPLE:

Ideas for sensory activities for home and classroom:

1. Stretchy resistance bands

2. Bouncing on exercise ball

3. Tactile sensory bins

4. Fidgets

5. Sensory bottles or tubes

6. Wall or chair push ups

7. Squeezing Play-Doh or thera-putty

8. Incorporate brain breaks

Please reference Recommended Resources 20 to 26 at the back of the book.

Conclusion

As your individual transitions back to school or work, it is key to remember that preparation will be paramount to their success. As discussed earlier in this workbook, attempt as much as possible to implement this structure two to three weeks in advance. Understand that, at first, your individual is going to be uncomfortable with the situation. However, through repetition and consistency, they will get used to their schedule again and their transition to school will be successful.

As we move forward and look to the future, there are many unknowns of how the COVID-19 virus will impact school and work settings. Other considerations that may need to be addressed using some strategies we have discussed are:

- Wearing face masks or other personal protective equipment (PPE)

- Wearing gloves

- Eating lunch at your desk; gatherings in cafeterias may not be allowed or restricted to small numbers

- No outside recess in large groups; may have recess in the classroom only

- No gathering in break areas at the workplace

- Special area instruction may take place in the classroom such as art, music, etc.

- Handwashing protocol

- Using hand sanitizer

- No interactions with other students outside of the child's classroom

- Meetings may only be held virtually

- Changes in the school calendar such as late start, partial days, continuing to do school virtually. This could also apply to the work environment

It will continue to be challenging as new regulations and protocols are developed over the coming months.

GOOD LUCK AND STAY SAFE!

Recommended Resources

SCHEDULING

1. Indiana University Bloomington website:
   A Social Narrative on Why I Use a Schedule https://www.iidc.
   indiana.edu/irca/resources/visual-supports/school.html
   Click the school button and scroll down to "Why I Use a
   Schedule."

2. And Next Comes L website: Free Printable Daily Visual Schedule
   https://www.andnextcomesl.com/2014/04/free-printable-
   daily-schedule.html

3. *Early Intervention and Autism: Real Life Questions, Real Life Answers* by Dr. James Ball

SOCIAL NARRATIVES

4. YouTube – ELF Kids Videos:
   I Eat With a Fork: Dinnertime Vocabulary and Pattern Practice
   https://www.youtube.com/watch?v=kKZ2_mraU4Y

5. YouTube – Phillipe Rose:
   Video Modeling: Meal Time
   https://www.youtube.com/watch?v=qLuDNpUSwrw

6. YouTube – BeLikeBuddy:
   Eating at the Table Social Story Video
   https://www.youtube.com/watch?v=dBc-83D5cNc

7. *Going Back to School After COVID-19* by Kristie Brown-Lofland

8. *No More Meltdowns* by Dr. Jed Baker

VIDEO MODELING

9. YouTube – Tiehole:
   How to Tie a Tie Video Model
   https://www.youtube.com/watch?v=xAg7z6u4NE8

10. *Video Modeling* by Steve Lockwood

REPETITION

11. *You Can't Make Me! Pro-Active Strategies for Positive Behavior Change in Children* by Dr. James Ball

SAFE PLACE/PERSON IN SCHOOL OR WORK

12. Natalie Lynn Kindergarten website: Creating a Classroom Calm Down Corner https://natalielynnkindergarten.com/creating-a-classroom-calm-down-corner/

13. *No More Meltdowns* by Dr. Jed Baker

14. *New Social Stories* by Carol Gray

CHAINING

15. Autism Classroom Resources website. A Teaching Strategy that can Save You Time: Chaining https://autismclassroomresources.com/a-teaching-strategy-that-can-save-you-time-chaining/

16. Accessible ABA website: Use Chaining and Task Analysis to Help Your Child with Autism https://accessibleaba.com/blog/chaining-task-analysis-autism

REINFORCEMENT/MOTIVATIONAL SYSTEM

17. Autism Behavior Therapy website: Free Printable First-and-Then Board https://autismbehaviourtherapy.com/free-printable-first-and-then-board/

18. StoryboardThat website: First Then Board Printable Template https://www.storyboardthat.com/storyboards/mon_shari/first-then-template

19. Teachers Pay Teachers website: First-Then Schedule Board Freebie
    https://www.teacherspayteachers.com/Product/First-Then-
    Schedule-Board-Freebie-713428

ANTICIPATE THEIR SENSORY NEEDS AND BE PREPARED

20. Noodle Nook website: COVID-19 Social Story FREE!
    http://www.noodlenook.net/covid-19-social-story-free/

21. PA Autism website: Wearing a Mask Social Story
    https://paautism.org/resource/wearing-mask-social-story/

22. Teachers Pay Teachers website: "We Wear Masks" – Coronavirus
    Social Story about Wearing a Mask
    https://www.teacherspayteachers.com/Product/We-Wear-Masks-
    Coronavirus-Social-Story-about-Wearing-a-Mask-5425981

23. Autism Little Learners website: Seeing People Wearing Masks
    Story
    https://www.autismlittlelearners.com/2020/04/seeing-people-
    wearing-masks-story.html

24. Autism Research Institute website: I Can Wear a Mask Social Story
    https://www.autism.org/wp-content/uploads/2020/04/I-can-wear-
    a-mask-1-1.pdf

25. YouTube – Jordan Drane:
    Wearing a Mask: A Social Narrative for Children
    https://www.youtube.com/watch?v=dYChl3jaVzA

26. YouTube – Illinois Autism Partnership:
    IAP – Masks Keep Us Safe
    https://www.youtube.com/watch?v=ipvbNzK4nXc

AUTHORS

DR. JIM BALL, a board-certified behavior analyst (BCBA-D), has been working in the private sector field of autism for over twenty-five years. In a variety of settings, he has provided educational, employment, and residential services to children and adults with autism.

Dr. Ball has lectured nationally and internationally, provided expert testimony, and published in the areas of early intervention, behavior, consultation services, social skills, technology, and trauma. He is a featured author and is on the advisory board for the *Autism Asperger's Digest* magazine. His triple award-winning book, *Early Intervention & Autism: Real-Life Questions, Real-Life Answers*, was released in February of 2008.

Dr. Ball's newest release, *You Can't Make Me*, sums up his years of working with behavioral challenges in individuals from eighteen months to eighty years of age.

Photo: BellowBlue

KRISTIE BROWN LOFLAND is an autism/educational consultant currently in private practice. Ms. Brown Lofland has previously worked in clinical, public school, and university settings. Ms. Brown Lofland has an extensive background in speech pathology, audiology, and the education and communication of individuals with autism spectrum disorders. She has made many presentations nationally and internationally in the area of communication and autism. Lofland holds a bachelor's degree in speech pathology from Indiana State University (1972), a master's degree in audiology from Indiana State University (1979), and a director of special education certificate from Indiana University (2003). She has held various offices and served on various committees with the Indiana Speech, Language and Hearing

Association. She was the recipient of honors of the Indiana Speech, Language, and Hearing Association for outstanding contributions in the field (2007). Ms. Lofland also received the "best in school advocacy" award from the Autism Society of Indiana (2007). She currently serves on the panel of professional advisors for the Autism Society of America, and is a member to the executive board for the Autism Society of Indiana.